Zen Traveller

BALI

~~~

A Quick Guide

by Gundi Gabrielle

First Edition Paperback: January 2017

ISBN-10: 1542462185
ISBN-13: 978-1542462181

The Cataloging-In-Publication Data is on file with the Library of Congress.

SassyZenGirl.com
SassyZenGirl.Group
DreamClientsOnAutopilot.com

Instagram.com/SassyZenGirl
Youtube.com/c/SassyZenGirl
Facebook.com/SassyZenGirl
Twitter.com/SassyZenGirl

*This is a **Zen Traveller** Guide*

TABLE OF CONTENT

For a full list of direct links to all resources mentioned in this book, please visit:

SassyZenGirl.com/Bali-Photos

Introduction

Bali is beautiful!

Quiet, serene, breathtaking, charming - magical...

That is, if you get away from the tourist crowds and overdeveloped settlements in the South - Kuta, Sanur, Seminyak etc.

Even Ubud is pretty crowded these days though still quite charming and certainly worth a visit.

Beyond Ubud though towards Candi Dasa and up the East and North Coast, it is almost like entering a different country.

Spectacular scenery - both mountains and ocean - and ever changing.

This is the Bali I would like to share with you in this book - the other side of Bali, away from all the parties, noise and commotion.

We will not cover any of the Southern tourist areas, but instead start in Ubud and then travel around the entire coastal line and inland into the Central and Northern mountains.

Most visitors never get that far - or don't even know what's out there - and that is sad as they are missing the most beautiful parts, the very parts that make Bali so special.

I love road trips and traveling through beautiful scenery in quiet, peace and solitude. While you can never completely avoid other people or a few tourist attractions in Bali, there are plenty of places to get away from it all - just be, breathe and enjoy the moment without too much chatter and rushing here and there. Just enjoying this amazingly beautiful island.

If this resonates with you, this book will be for you. If instead you are looking for parties, shopping and crowded beaches, you will be disappointed as I will not cover those at all.

Plenty of other publications for that.

This book is meant as an overview to help you get oriented. To see what's where and then plan according to your preferences and time frame. It is **not** an in-depth *Lonely Planet* type book.

A picture says more than a thousand words and nowhere more so than in travel.

I included a few photos throughout the text and created additional color photo pages on my travel blog at:

SassyZenGirl.com/Bali-Photos

Links for resources can also be found there.

All maps were created with *Google Maps*. Direct links can be found on the above page, allowing you to adjust the itinerary to your needs and preferences, send it to your iphone as a gps or print it out.

Where applicable, I will include some of my own recommendations for accommodation, transport etc. - I do not receive compensation for mentioning these outfits, but am sharing personal experiences that have been quite wonderful. They may or may not relate to your travel needs.

Now......if you are ready to explore some fantastic beauty, stillness, nature and true Balinese hospitality, let's begin!

Chapter 1 - Beautiful Bali

Orientation

Bali is not a big island and yet, it takes several days to drive all around. You will land in the **South at Denpasar Airport**, and that's also where most of the crowded tourist areas are - Kuta, Seminyak, Sanur, Nusa Dua etc.

The **East and North Coast** offer exquisite diving and snorkeling with beautiful coral reefs to explore. The beaches are mostly black. Life is relaxed and quiet here with expansive coconut tree vegetation along the coast, and lush rain forests inland towards the mountains. The main towns/villages are Candi Dasa and Amed in the East and Singaraja, Lovina and Pemuteran in the North.

West Bali National Park (**"Bali Barat"**) along the very far North West Coast presents an entirely different scenery and vegetation with monsoon forest, savannah and mangroves, and offers easy access to East Java and the Java Volcanoes. The **West Coast** around Medewi and Canggu is famous for surfing.

Turning **inland** you will find gorgeous mountain ranges. Lush rain forests, opulent rice terraces and towering volcanos with massive lakes. A fantastic scenery with great hiking options and many quiet spots. Munduk and Bedugul are the main villages/towns in the **northern mountains**. Ubud - also Bali's main cultural centre - in the **central mountains**, an hour North of Denpasar.

The three major **volcanoes** are *Mount Batur/Kintamani* and *Mount Bratan* in the **North**, both with large crater lakes, and *Mount Agung*, Bali's highest peak, in the **East**.

Here is a map for a first overview (next page):

Balinese People & Culture

The Balinese People are Wonderful!

They are incredibly warm and welcoming, and I would recommend staying at a local guest house/homestay once in a while to get a real feel for the island and her people.

Bali is mostly Hindu with a few sprinklings of Muslims and Buddhists - and it's a very unique brand of Hinduism.

Very sweet, lots of little ceremonies, completely interwoven with people's lives. Very loving and open and yet very deeply determined on their spiritual path. At hotels, you will often be told that a certain staff member isn't available, because he or she is "at a ceremony" - and there is always some type of ceremony every day.

Most Balinese never leave their village or region in their entire life. I was often asked by Northerners what things were like in the South and vice versa. Quite amazing, given that it's not a large island...

For centuries, people stayed in their villages, learned the crafts of their parents and continued the traditions. With the younger generation, this is gradually changing, but very slowly.

People here are chill, happy and friendly - content with their lives and where they are - and why wouldn't they, living in such a paradise?

Traveling in Bali as a woman is very safe. Balinese women are pretty much equal and have careers of their own, and you are always treated with respect.
In remote areas and traditional villages it is advisable not to dress in super skimpy shorts and tank tops - out of respect for people and their traditions.
No one will bother or harass you, they will be just as welcoming, but in remote villages that have little interactions with tourists, it will be much appreciated.

Also, in temples both men and woman have to wear a little sarong to cover the legs. You can always rent one for a small fee or bring one yourself. The only country I'm aware of where this also applies to men…..

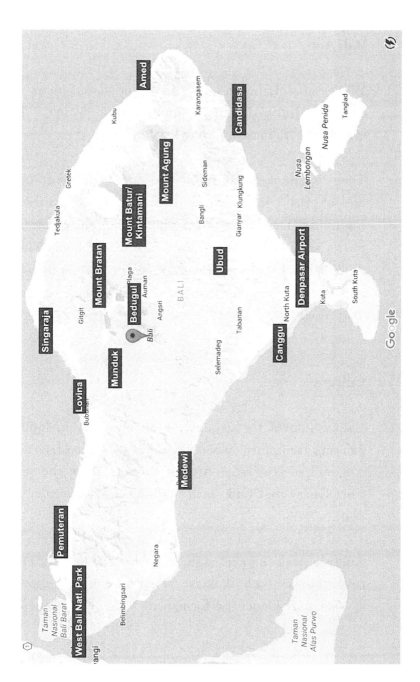

Bali Aga

While most Balinese are said to be descendants of several Hindu-Javanese immigration waves, the indigenous Balinese are called Bali Aga.

Their culture and way of life is distinctly different, and life in Bali Aga villages still follows the ancient traditions. The best known villages are the *Tenganan* near Candi Dasa and *Trunyan* near Kintamani. While the first is a popular tourist destination, *Trunyan* is to be approached with some caution as I will describe in *Day Trips from Ubud*.

Culture

Bali is known for exquisite craftsmanship, including painting, sculpture, woodcarving and handcrafts. You will find several large Artisan Villages along the way from Sanur to **Ubud**, each focusing on one particular craft.

Another well known sight are the elaborate dance performances with Balinese percussion music, known as *Gamelan*. Dance performances - usually combined with a Balinese dinner - can be observed all over the island.

Balinese Cuisine is unique and distinct from Indonesian cuisine. Favorite dishes include *Lawar, Bebek Betutu* and *Celeng Guling* as well as *Nasi Campur* (a Balinese variation of the Indonesian *Nasi Goreng* which you can also find all over the island).

Communication

Language

Bali has its own language, different from Indonesian though people usually speak and understand both.

Most Balinese speak at least basic English - quite in contrast to the rest of Asia - so you usually won't have problems getting around or asking directions etc.

The locals here love to talk with international visitors and find out where you are from and how you like Bali, and domestic tourists love to pose for selfies with a foreigner. I met a group of Javanese school girls at one of the Northern Temples and they couldn't have been more excited, taking selfies for about 10 minutes, interviewing me (sometimes using Google translate...) and giggling the whole time. I felt like a celebrity...;-)

In other words - you feel very welcome here!

Internet/Mobile Service

Internet is getting much better with many parts now having fiber optics though you will face the occasional outage or shakiness. Hotels and guest houses will often advertise "free fiber optics Wi-fi", so if that's important to you, be sure to ask. Wi-fi at hotels is usually free.

Cell/mobile phones work without problem almost everywhere. I even had to make an urgent business call once on *Mount Agung* and had no problem getting through via Skype.

You can buy prepaid SIM cards with 4G/LTE data plans right at the airport. These are the 2 main options:

Telkomsel - more expensive, but better signal
Indosat - cheaper, and still a decent signal

Accommodation

Aside from hotels and resorts, Bali offers two very unique forms of accommodation: Homestays & Bali Villas.

You can find both through the regular booking sites. I like **Booking.com**, because I don't have to pre-pay and rarely need to provide a credit card to secure the reservation. With homestays be aware though that cash payment is usually expected.

Homestays

Become part of a Balinese family. Privately run Guest Houses - or "Homestays" as they are called here - are usually sparkling clean, beautifully furnished and decorated, and often featuring a small terrace. Most come with private baths (if you are lucky even an outdoor bath which is refreshing in the morning), free Wi-fi, AC and breakfast. You get to meet real Balinese at their homes, because many of the guest houses are family run on the owner's properties.

I had the best banana pancakes *ever* at this cute little guest house in Pemuteran while enjoying amazing mountain views on my private terrace......

You can easily find nice Homestays for just $20 a night, including all the above, as long as you stay away from the High Season, which is July/August/September and Christmas/New Year.

This was the room to go with the pancakes - simple, but clean and nice, and look at the lovely flower petal greeting on the bed......

Bali Villas

Bali is famous for her beautiful villas and you can find many wonderful options on **Booking.com** and **AirBnB.**

I was invited as a travel writer to four unique properties featuring luxury villas and will share those options as we travel around the island.

Villas are more expensive, but can offer privacy for families or groups and usually come with kitchens, pools - and often staff....

Transportation

Getting around the Island

There is no public transport as such. No trains or bus lines.

Instead, there are four main options to get around the island:

#1 - Rent a car

If you are good with left side driving and ready for a bit of traffic chaos in the South, renting a car will give you the most flexibility, but there are a few things to consider:

Traffic cops are notorious for targeting tourists in rental cars and scooters around tourist sites, charging exorbitant fines for even the smallest infractions and you really don't have much recourse. Similar situation if you get in an accident. You might have to fork out several hundred Dollars for "medical expenses" and again, there is not much you can do, but pay.

For better prices, don't hire a car at the airport (Hertz etc.) but ask your guesthouse or hotel to arrange one for you. Rates start as low as 100,000 IDR (less than $10) per day, more with AC and insurance. Better rates for long term rentals.

You will need an International Drivers License for both cars and scooters.

#2 - Rent a Car with a Driver

The most common option. While I normally love road trips and driving myself, this time I found a great driver and would recommend that way of traveling, especially for long distances.

Local drivers know the island inside out. They can adjust the itinerary to your specific preferences - in my case, the quiet country roads with beautiful nature and scenery. You don't have to deal with parking, gas/petrol, insurance, traffic cops or finding your way - though Google Maps is pretty reliable as a GPS.

A driver will usually cost between $45-60/day, depending on the length of route, hours etc., but as a rough estimate. This includes gas/petrol, all parking fees and the driver/guide. They can also transport you between different parts of the island, even one-way.

I can recommend Awa from *Bali Candi Dasa Tours* (balicandidasatour@gmail.com) and Gede as a wonderful driver. Awa gave me fair prices and made an effort to tailor make my trip. Gede Lausen is one of his best drivers. Fun, well informed with good English and very sensitive to your particular preferences. He always picked the lovely country roads for me and suggested additional stops along the way that were very enjoyable and not necessarily part of a regular tour.

#3 - Shuttle Buses

Connect most major routes/villages and are quite cheap. They only take you from A to B though. No stops in between at attractions etc. or enjoying nature and scenery.

Perama Tours (PeramaTour.com) is the best known outfit and offers daily shuttle buses all over the island, also in combination with ferry service to Lombok.

#4 - Scooters/Mopeds

Scooters are really fun!! - If you only have a backpack and love a fresh breeze, this is definitely the way to go - and also surprisingly cheap (about $5-7 per day).

Everyone has a scooter in Bali and you get everywhere quickly.

For longer distances around the island it might be better to go by bus or car and then rent a scooter at your guest house/hotel to explore the surrounding areas. Also, keep in mind that some parts of Bali are very mountainous and not everyone will enjoy driving winding serpentines on a scooter (or their stomach…).

Once again, be aware, that traffic cops love to target tourists, especially if you are not wearing a helmet and be sure to have insurance cover.

#5 - Taxis

Taxis can only be found in the South and drivers will frequently try to overcharge you. Be it a "minimum charge" (which should be 5,000 IDR), to not employing a meter, charging "pick-up fees" or not having proper change - I've seen it all and it's quite annoying.

Another reason to avoid the South as it is the only region where heavy tourism has jaded some of the locals, and you won't always find the integrity and friendliness that is otherwise so typical of Balinese people.

If you do take a taxi, always make sure there is a meter or pre-negotiate the fare. Whatever they offer, settle for half, then you are usually in the right ballpark (you can ask at your hotel/guesthouse what the proper fare should be). Walking away is a very effective negotiation strategy, btw….;-)

Blue Bird (BluebirdGroup.com) is one of the good taxi companies.

Climate

Bali is just 8 degrees South of the equator and has a fairly even tropical climate year round. Temperatures are around 30°C (ca. 85°F) with high humidity - cooler in the higher mountain regions.

There are two seasons:

- Dry season: April to September

- Rainy season: October-March

Also good to know: Tourist High Season is from July to September and over the Christmas/New Year's Holidays. Best to avoid those times. Prices will be higher and, of course, it will be a lot more crowded.

The best months to visit are May/June and late September.

During rainy season you can expect a daily heavy rain shower or thunderstorm, usually in the afternoon, and then the sun comes out again.

I find heavy, tropical rain quite wonderful! There is something magnificent and cleansing about that awesome power of nature, part of the cycle of life. Not depressing and gloomy as it can be in colder climates, but that's just me....

Safety

Bali is very safe overall. In the busy tourist regions of the South you should be a little careful with pickpockets. Also, taxi drivers will frequently try to overcharge you, but rarely violent crimes.

As a woman I never felt threatened or endangered in any way - quite the opposite, it was one of the safest places I ever traveled in.

Hawkers & "Guides"

One unfortunate evil in the tourist hotspots are hawkers. You will get pestered everywhere , but if you are firm, they will usually leave you alone and be happy to just chat. It is not the aggressive pushiness I have seen in India for example where hawkers and professional beggars can be downright rude.
People here just need to survive, so they will be persistent, but they respect if you are firm.

Hawkers mostly disappear once you leave the busy South. There were a few in Lovina, certainly *Tanah Lot* and *Kintamani*, but most other parts - even well known attractions like *Jatiluwih Rice Terrace*, *Bedugul Lake* and *Tirta Gangga* - where remarkably free of this nuisance.

Another problem you occasionally encounter are so-called "guardians" (guides) that try to pressure you into hiring their over-priced services. The worst I encountered at *Besakih, Mother Temple* where several "guardians" insisted I had to use their services or I could not see the temple.

Fortunately, my driver Gede had warned me and assured me that I didn't need a guide to enter the temple grounds. As a seasoned traveler and "tough New York" I firmly held my ground, but they were very persistent and even tried to take my ticket. So beware....

Again, no one is violent here and you don't have to worry about causing a scene - just be firm and keep walking and you will be fine.

Visa

Most countries don't need a visa to enter Indonesia. Instead you get a free visa exempt stamp at immigration. This is valid for 30 days and cannot be extended. You must leave the country and then come back.

Alternately, you can apply for a 60 day visa ahead of time. From many travelers I was warned not to apply for the 60 day visa from within Bali as it can take a long time to process. Instead, apply abroad at an Indonesian Embassy before flying to Bali and it will usually be much easier.

If you overstay even by a day, you will be charged a hefty fine and might have trouble entering the next time - and they *do* check when you leave. So really count the days carefully and include arrival and departure days to avoid any problems when you leave.

Money

Currency

Currency is the Indonesian Rupiah (IDR). An easy way to convert into US Dollar is: cutting off 4 zeros and take 75% of the rest. As an example: 600,000 IRD = 45 USD

Exchange rates will fluctuate, of course, but as a rough guide, this is quite helpful.

Credit Cards

Credit cards are a little more common in Bali than other Asian countries, but mostly in the South.

At guest houses and small stores you will always have to pay cash, also for most tours, chauffeurs, taxis, admissions etc.

Large hotels and supermarkets are the only places where you can reliably pay with credit card, otherwise, assume cash only.

I strongly dislike cash because of high ATM and cash advance bank fees (easily a combined $15-20 per advance) and the lack of expense tracking. And of course, lost mileage or cash back points. But that's just the way it is in most of Asia, so it's good to be prepared and get a larger sum of cash when you arrive.

Interestingly, in South Africa I could pay with credit cards everywhere, even in small rural villages, but not so in Asia.

As for ATMs - be sure to pick a major bank ATM and try to use it during office hours, in case it doesn't work properly or keeps your card. I never had a problem, but was told it could occasionally happen and that's not something you want to deal with on a Sunday.....

Chapter 2 - Ubud & Central Mountains

Ubud

Ubud is lovely!

Well known, of course, especially after being featured in the movie "Eat, Pray, Love", and highly frequented by tourists, yet never losing its charm and appeal.

Ubud is the cultural centre of Bali and should be part of your itinerary though it won't be the quietest of places.

Coming up from the South, you will pass through a number of "Artisan Villages". Their craftsmanship is impressive, just be aware that these places are geared towards tourists and will heavily try to sell you. If you want a souvenir or gift, they can be wonderful, if not, the constant haggling can be a little tiresome.

"Downtown" Ubud

Ubud is small and easily walkable. There is a Royal Palace in the center that you can start your journey

from and then just explore the lovely side streets, cafes, restaurants, galleries and shops.

Really lovely and a very chill, laid back atmosphere.

Monkey Forest

A well known attraction at the outskirts of Ubud is *"Monkey Forest"* (MonkeyForestUbud.com). A large forested area with a monkey sanctuary and many walking paths to see the joyful menagerie.

The monkeys are free - and they roam everywhere.

You can buy a few bananas to feed them, but you won't have them long as the monkeys are quite pushy and will climb all over you and into your bags. So best not to....

Without bananas it will be a much more pleasant experience and you can really enjoy their play and interactions.

You will see monkeys of all sizes and they might be right next to you or walk in front of you, jump through the trees or sit on the fences and play.

It's fun!

Rice Fields

The most wonderful "attraction" around Ubud are the rice fields and lovely country side. You can rent a scooter or bicycle and simply go. Or just walk on the many pathways.

A nice spot is *Sari Organik*'s **Warung Boɒag Maliah,** an organic restaurant/cafe in the midst of rice fields and river valleys. Beautiful scenery, wonderful food, all produced on the surrounding organic farm.

For accommodation, you can choose Ubud center or the surrounding villages. There are plenty of options in all price ranges, including Bali Villas.

Last time I stayed at **Suara Air Villas** (SuaraAir.com) in the village of *Benjar Melayang*. Total quiet and solitude, my own villa with pool, lush green rain forests and rice fields all around. Heaven…..

Goa Gajah - Elephant Cave

Among the attractions around Ubud, *Goa Gajah* is the most famous. There are no elephants here, but rather one of the most impressive archaeological sites in Bali, dating back to the 11th century. Located in Bedulu Village, 6km out of central Ubud, *Goa Gajah* was built as a spiritual place for meditation.

The grounds are gorgeous and feature both Hindu and Buddhist influences. At the Southern end you can walk through beautiful rice fields and along two small streams leading up to Petanu River. A river junction like this was considered sacred and as such *Goa Gajah* was built as a hermetic site for mediation and prayer.

Campuhan Ridge Walk

A free and easy nature trek with gorgeous hillside vistas of the region and namesake valley. The walk starts from

Gunung Lebah Temple and is usually not very busy - you might actually have it all to yourself…..

Museums

There are a number of unique museums in and around Ubud - most notably the following three:

- *Setia Darma Masks & Puppets House*: tries to preserve some of Indonesia's most colorful treasures. Currently houses over 1,000 masks and 4,000 puppets from all over Indonesia, Africa, China, Latin America and Europe in 5 traditional wooden Balinese pavilions and Javanese "joglo" and "limasan" houses.

- *Blanco Renaissance Museum* (BlancoMuseum.com) something of an unofficial landmark in Ubud. The house and studio of flamboyant Filipino artist Don Antonio Blanco. Located on a hilltop overlooking *Campuhan Valley*, the museum houses many of the artist's paintings, collages and illustrated poetry, as well as lithographic artwork of his favorite subject: nude Balinese women.

- *Agung Rai Museum of Art (ARMA) (ArmaBali.com):* features a large collection of Balinese artwork. Located in Pengosekan, 3 km south of Ubud center.

Sidemen

A secret tip among experienced Bali travelers is Sideman (pronounced si-da-men). A quieter alternative to Ubud with more traditional, local charm. Situated 90 minutes North East of Ubud towards Mount Agung, this lovely local spot is spread out over an enchanting valley with beautiful rice fields and terraced hills - basically, Ubud without the crowds.

Day Trips from Ubud

Day Trip 1 - Kintamani Volcano

The most popular Day Trip from Ubud (and anywhere in the South) goes up to *Kintamani Volcano* via *Tegalalang Rice Terrace.*

If you are coming from the South or the airport, you can also include *Tegenungan Waterfall* and the Artisan Villages on the way from Sanur.

It is a typical tourist route - ALL the tour companies go there, so unless you leave early you will be inundated with crowds. *Kintamani* is an amazing site though and certainly worth a visit and possibly an overnight stay.

There is a quieter way to include *Kintamani* which I cover in the **Amed to Lovina Chapter**.

Tegenungan Waterfall

To be honest, *Tegenungan Waterfall* was nice, but not *that* impressive. Unless you have never seen a waterfall, I wouldn't do a loop South if you are starting this trip from Ubud. If you are coming up from the South, however, it will be right along the way, so a nice stop. Just be sure to arrive in the morning, while the tourist crowds are still busy in the Artisan Villages.

Tegalalang Rice Terrace

Tegalalang Rice Terrace was lovely and well worth a stop - again, try to get there early, definitely before noon to avoid the crowds.

There is a nice cafe/restaurant where we stopped for coffee - with amazing views. It can also be a nice breakfast stop.

Be sure to try "Bali Coffee" at least once. It's delicious!

Tegalalang does not compare with *Jatiluwih Rice Terrace* in the North. *Jatiluwih* is absolutely spectacular and will be covered in the **Northern Mountains Chapter,** but if you don't have the time to go all the way up there, *Tegelalang* will give you a nice impression of a Balinese Rice terrace and some wonderful photo ops.

Gunung Kawi Shrines

If you leave the main highway and take some of the lovely country roads, you will come across *Gunung Kawi*, one of Bali's oldest and largest ancient monuments. 10 shrines - memorials cut out of the rock face, dating back to the 11th century and thought to be representing royalties of the era.

For me the nicest part of the whole trip. Few tourists, a quiet, peaceful atmosphere and beautiful grounds surrounded by rice terraces and a mighty river.

Kintamani Volcano

Kintamani Volcano - or *Mount Batur* as it is also called - offers spectacular views and various hiking and trekking options, especially if you stay overnight.

The views of *Batur Lake*, surrounded by mountain ranges are magnificent. You can also take a winding road down and along the lake shore to *Toya Bungkah* and a collection of hot springs. The latter is also a popular spot among trekkers to spend the night before hiking up *Mount Batur* and watch the sunrise.

There are three main villages here: Penelokan, Batur and Kintamani with Penelokan offering the most stunning views from the southernmost crater rim. A voluptuous blend of dark lava slopes, black molten rocks, lush green vegetation and the turquoise-green colors of *Batur Lake*.

It can be crowded and there are a lot of hawkers at the view points, but it is an amazing site and well worth including. A particularly stunning drive leads up from the East Coast and would be my preferred choice to visit *Kintamani* - more on that in the **Amed to Lovina Chapter.**

And excellent tour company in Kintamani, run by a Dutch Australian couple is *C-Bali Canoeing & Cultural (Cycling) Tours* (C-Bali.com). They offer very unusual tours up to traditional villages, canoeing across the massive lake and sunrise treks up to Mount Batur. *Not* - the usual tourist stuff.....

Trunyan Cemetery

A somewhat infamous attraction near Kintamani is the Bali Aga/Trunyan Cemetery. It's on the list of "Things NOT to do in Bali" and if that appeals to you, by all means, go for it....;-)

The cemetery is unusual because the Trunyan people - part of the indigenous Bali Aga tribes - don't bury or cremate their dead, but instead leave them on the cemetery grounds to gradually "fade" away.

You get to see skulls and skeletons and there might be a strange smell - it has quite a fascination for some people....

Unfortunately, the Trunyan residents are known to be exceptionally pushy and charge outrageous prices for the short boat ride across the lake.

As soon as you arrive, you will be surrounded with demands for "donations" and for the short 10 min boat trip over to the cemetery fares start at 1 Million IDR (ca. $75) per Person - an exorbitant amount.

That's not all though. Once you get to the middle of the lake they might demand even more payment for "gas" and refuse to continue until you pay…..

In other words, this could be a very expensive adventure with rather little return from what I've been told. The cemetery is very small and apparently not that impressive. But see for yourself if you are up for an unusual experience. - *That*, you will certainly get…;-)

You can read up on TripAdvisor - there are plenty of stories describing a Trunyan visit. One way to avoid all the above is to book a tour from Ubud. Most of the regular tour companies are not allowed to guide tours at Trunyan, but I've heard excellent things about Yansu from ***Beautiful Bali Tours*** (BeautifulBaliTours.com) so I would recommend booking through him. He apparently comes from the village and can avoid all the haggling.

Day Trip 2 - Besakih Temple

Another favorite day trip from Ubud is *Besakih Mother Temple* on the slopes of Mount Agung. We will journey there in the next chapter on our way to Candi Dasa and the Bali East Coast.

Cat-Poo-Cino

Luwak Coffee - or one of the Top 10 Cruelest Animal Attractions in the World

The region around Kintamani is plum with lovely coffee and tea plantations and a visit can be a wonderful experience.

Unfortunately, the region is also famous for the most expensive coffee in the world - *Luwak* coffee - made from the poo (you heard right) of wild cats = civets that are known to eat coffee berries. Those berries "digest" in the civets' stomach and can be turned into delicacy coffee - or so they claim.

I once had *Luwak* coffee before I knew what it was - you don't expect cat poo after all, when offered prime coffee - and it was sour and bitter, quite awful actually.

Sadly, the civets are mass produced for coffee production, held in tiny cages - often many crowded together where they hurt each other and only fed coffee berries which is one sided and very unhealthy for them.

If you love animals, please don't participate in anything that says "Cat Poo Cino" or "Luwak Coffee" - it has been rated as one of the *Top 10 cruelest animal attractions in the world*.

Instead, you can still do a tour of a coffee plantation and a free tasting which is fun and very informative - and then refuse the *Luwak* coffee for which they will charge extra. You might even point out why you are refusing it.

That's the only way to stop this brutal practice: if money no longer flows and tourists show their disgust at the practice.

The plantations offer many other coffee and tea brands that you can enjoy without participating in the cruelty.

Chapter 3 - Ubud to Candi Dasa

The road trip from Ubud to Candi Dasa via *Besakih Mother Temple* offers breathtaking views, beautiful countryside and a mix of both mountains and ocean views.

It feels like entering a different country and will allow you to leave crowded tourist Bali behind once and for all. For the first time you will get a sense of that peaceful serenity that is so typical for life in Bali.

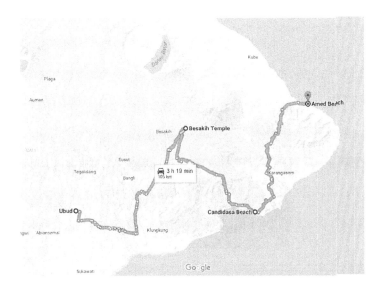

From Ubud you take the road to *Besakih*, the "Mother" Temple on the slopes of *Mount Agung*, the principal volcano and highest mountain in Bali.

Besakih Temple

Besakih is a complex of 26 temples and the largest and most important in all of Bali. The exact origins of the temple are unknown, but it almost certainly dates from prehistoric times.

A series of eruptions from Mount Agung, in 1963 killed almost 1,700 people, but miraculously missed the temple by just a few meters, forever endowing it with special significance for the Balinese people.

The drive up the mountain is stunning, offering gorgeous vistas in many places.

The temple grounds are beautiful, too - very impressive actually, but unfortunately haunted by a syndicate of so-called "guardians" who will try to force you to pay exorbitant guide fees simply to walk up a few stairs and see the temple.

As I already mentioned, don't fall for them. You don't need them and they have no right to harass you. Just be firm and keep walking and you will be fine.

From *Besakih*, take the country roads via Putung Village to Candi Dasa.

It is absolutely beautiful!

Along the way are several options for white water rafting which is becoming a bigger industry in Bali, but mostly just gorgeous countryside and magnificent views, especially once the ocean appears on the horizon - quite a moment!

Chapter 4 - Candi Dasa

Candi Dasa (pronounced Chahn-dee Dasa) is a sleepy little town. Lush with coconut trees, breezy and pleasant. A beautiful spot to spend a few days.

The white, sandy beaches - once the town's greatest attraction - are sadly eroded. In the 1980s, a sudden boom in beach bungalow and hotel construction caused the coral reef to be removed to produce lime for cement. A fatal decision as it allowed the power of the Lombok strait to erode the beaches - and they never recovered.

Concrete sea walls now protect from further erosion and the waters are calm and good for snorkeling as a result. There are a few pockets of sand though they often disappear during high tide.

Don't let this keep you from Candi Dasa though. It is still a beautiful spot and very relaxing with a number of interesting attractions in the near vicinity, including a few beautiful beaches.

The town center is adorned with a lotus covered lagoon right in front of the ocean.

Sites around Candi Dasa

Goa Lawah Bat Cave & Temple

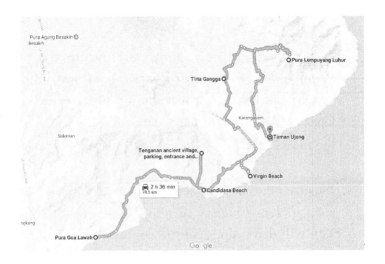

Located 20km South of Candi Dasa in the village of Pasinggahan, *Goa Lawah* is one of the major attractions in Bali. As such it can be crowded, but it is so unusual that it makes for a fun stop along the way, especially if you drive up from Denpasar - it's right near the highway.

Goa Lawah means "bat cave" and houses thousands of chirping bats that you can see flying around. Only priests can enter the cave, but you can easily see and photograph them from the front.

Virgin Beach

20 minutes North of Candi Dasa, lies lovely, secluded *Virgin Beach* (*Pasir Putih* Beach) - the last white sand beach you will see for a while if you travel up the East Coast. Well known, especially after being featured in the movie "Eat, Pray, Love", but not very crowded.

Be sure not the miss the hand painted signs off the main road in *Perasi Village*, turning right towards the ocean. You will drive along a little country road that gets a bit rocky and rough at times and then park your car and walk the rest down a hill (a 5 minute walk - I was asked that question 3 times by other visitors when I came back up....;-)

There are a few small warungs (food stands) that also rent out sun lounges and some fishermen offering boat trips on outrigger type canoes.

Bali Aga Villages

Tenganan Pegringsingan and *Tenganan Dauh Tukad* are two Bali Aga Villages near Candi Dasa. The Bali Aga are the indigenous Balinese and still live their traditional way of life, deeply rooted in ancient customs and traditions.

Tourism is a major source of income for both villages and very obviously so, but *Pegringsingan* in particular, is quite pretty and the way of life is interesting to observe. There is no individual ownership of property, and women participate equally in communal share and inheritance.

The villages are famous for their ceremony of *Usaba Sumbah* in June, involving fights with sharp pandan leaves - *Perang Pandan* - between young village men as a coming of age ritual and *Ayunan*, a large wooden ferris wheel carrying young women.

The Tenganan are also renowned for their textile traditions, in particular, the *geringsing*, a complex double ikat, believed to have mystical and healing powers.

Again, touristy, yes, and residents very actively try to sell their products, but so unique and interesting that it's still worth a visit.

Tirta Gangga Royal Water Garden

Tirta Gangga impresses with a maze of pools and fountains surrounded by a lush garden with stone carvings and statues.

It is beautiful!

The garden was built in 1948 by the Raja (King) of Karangasem and the name means "Water from the Ganges", India's Holy River, a site of reverence for the Hindu Balinese.

A number of polygonal stepping stones in the first pond allow visitors to step on the water and traverse the pond.

You can also take a bath here.

The temple was destroyed almost entirely by the eruption of Mount Agung in 1963 and has since been lovingly re-built and restored to its original royal magnificence.

The area around *Tirta Gangga* features lush rice terraces and beautiful ocean views on one side and Mount Agung on the other. A beautiful drive with many places to stop along the way.

Taman Ujung Water Palace

The sister site to *Tirta Gangga*, located right by the ocean. It was also built by the late Raja of Karangasem and almost destroyed by lava ashes following the eruption of Mount Agung in 1963 and an earthquake in 1979. Like *Tirta Gangga*, it was carefully restored over the years and is a stunning site!

"Ujung" means "extremity" in Indonesian and refers to the enormous size of the park at 10 ha., one of the largest sites in all of Bali.

The park features a combination or Balinese and European architecture with three large ponds connected by elegant bridges and pathways. The main pool was not intended as a royal bath, interestingly, but instead as a place of punishment for proponents of black magic or witchcraft...

Lempuyang Temple

A trip to *Lempuyang Temple* can easily be a day trip of its own. It is one of the oldest and most impressive temples in all of Bali and requires climbing over 1700 stairs (yes…..) to get to the actual temple! At least 2 hours each way.

Located at the top of Mount Lempuyang, the views are stunning even from the first level with lush green mountain forests providing some shade. A number of attractions along the way - mostly smaller temples and large hordes of grey long-tailed Macaques - will keep you entertained during your climb.

There is a spiritual aspect to the ascent. The locals believe that pilgrims with a heavy heart will never make it to the top. You also shouldn't complain while walking…..

Chapter 5 - Amed

Amed is a chill little fishing village. Very basic, no fancy restaurants or glamorous board walks. Simple.

But quite charming in its own way.

Amed together with neighboring Tulamben is the most famous diving spot in the region with beautiful coral reefs and a legendary ship wreck. Most tourists here are divers - not surprisingly.

Amed was the first place where I saw black beaches, quite different from the sandy white at *Virgin Beach* near Candi Dasa.

It's not a "pretty" place, but pleasant and laid back and fun to spend a few daya.

Traditional Salt Farms

Amed is famous for traditional salt farming, still done by hand. The village of Purwakerti on the way into Amed offers visitors to observe the process.

Sea water is poured into dugout halves of coconut tree trunks along the coast and left to dry under the sun. The farmers then harvest the remaining salt crystals which you can purchase in little packets.

Diving

Amed has special significance for me, because I had my first Scuba dive here, something that had been on my bucket list for a long time.

I found a wonderful local instructor in Imade from *Dream Divers Bali* (DreamDiversBali.com) Imade was born in Amed and has known these waters all his life - and with a name like "Dream Divers" why would you go anywhere else...;-)

Gili Islands can also be reached from Amed. Ferries go daily, both to Gili and Lombok.

Tulamben

Another fishing village and popular diving spot, 30 minutes up the coast. Features a famous ship wreck, the USS Liberty. The cargo ship sank following a torpedo hit from a Japanese submarine in 1942 and now lies 30 meters off the coastline. A favorite playground for divers from all around the world.

Mountain Hiking & a Gorgeous Coastline

Aside from diving, you can hike into Mount Agung or rent a scooter and drive South around the rugged coastline. Peaceful bays, clear waters and breathtaking ocean views...

Near the entrance, *Jemeluk Viewpoint* offers great vistas of the bay. Set upon a hill, this scenic stopover provides beautiful photo ops and a few shaded gazebos for a rest stop or picnic.

A Coffee Shop with a View

I discovered a new coffee shop in Amed - "The Cup" - with excellent Wi-fi. Set on the 3rd floor of a building with ocean vistas, you can enjoy a nice breeze, beautiful

views and sunsets, tasty dishes and Italian style coffees - as well as the fastest Wi-fi in town!

You can find it across the street from *Dream Divers Bali* in the village center.

The Nutella pancakes and juices were amazing!

The only thing they didn't offer - ironically - was Bali coffee....

Chapter 6 - East Coast: Amed to Lovina

The drive from Amed to Lovina takes about 2-3 hours though I would recommend taking time along the way.

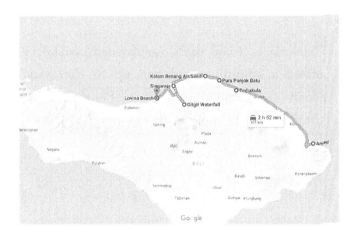

The whole East Coast is lush with coconut trees and jungle. You feel relaxed just looking at it!

The drive is beautiful with lovely little villages and quiet beaches along the way. In the off season you don't need to pre-reserve accommodations. Just go and see where you like it and stay a while.

Plenty to choose from at very low rates.

Tejakula

Tejakula is a laid back, uncrowded coastal village and offers a stunning road trip up to *Kintamani Volcano/ Crater Lake*, and the village of Penelokan overlooking the blackened smoking *Batur Crater*. The winding road

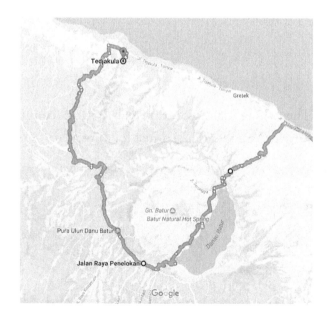

leads up through clove and citrus plantations and some pretty breathtaking views.

You can also detour from the highway coming up from Amed and do a loop, rather than driving the same route in both directions.

Pura Ponjok Batu Temple

Heading North from Tejakula you will pass a picturesque cliffside temple called *Pura Ponjok Batu*. According to local folklore, the temple was founded by the 16th-century priest Nirartha after he rescued a shipwrecked crew, and rocks on the nearby promontory began emitting light. A small boat-shaped shrine can be seen in the sea in front of the temple.

Yeh Sanih

20 minutes further up the road, in the village of Sanih, you can cool off in a cold-water pool fed with natural spring water - *Yeh Sanih*. The water comes from underground rivers that originate in *Batur Lake*, the volcanic crater lake up on *Kintamani*.

Yeh Sanih - or *Air Sanih* as it is also called (air=water in Indonesian, yeh=water in Balinese) - is very popular among Balinese. Even my driver Gede had just been there with his brother over the weekend. So not the typical tourist spot and beautifully situated right on the ocean.

Singaraja

Singaraja used to be the capital of Bali and is the second largest city on the island after Denpasar. Guide books will often praise it as interesting, but I found it mostly noisy and crowded. A bit of a shock after the remoteness and peace everywhere else, so I did not spend any time there.

There is a nice Dutch colonial waterfront, a library, museums and a few temples, but if you don't like crowds and noisy places, you probably won't enjoy Singaraja very much.

It is, however, the only stop aside from the South where you can stock up on certain necessities and find a regular supermarket and shopping mall. I had been dying to find dental floss ever since I left Ubud and neither Candi Dasa, nor Amed, nor anywhere else along the coast could I find it! People didn't understand what I was talking about and once they did usually started giggling - but no dental floss......

So if you forgot something or ran out, Singaraja will be the place to find it.

Gitgit Waterfall

Before you head to Lovina Beach, you can include a little detour to *Gitgit Waterfall*, the most famous waterfall in Bali.
Gitgit will be described more in **Northern Mountains Chapter**. The detour takes about 30 minutes each way.

Chapter 7 - Lovina Beach

The name "Lovina" stands for a string of little villages along the North coast that are all grouped together as *Lovina Beach*.

Lovina is the main tourist location on the North Coast, but by far not as busy as the South, though you will see the occasional hawker.

Beaches are black everywhere on the North coast, and diving and snorkeling are the main activities for travelers, aside from dolphins.

Dolphin Cruises

Lovina's top attraction are dolphin "cruises" early in the morning - *not* as fun as you might think…..

They are overcrowded with overnight tourists from the South, and the only available boat option are small, narrow fishing boats with rock hard benches and deafening motor noise for 2 hours straight (the trip out to the dolphins takes an hour each way). Be sure to bring ear plugs or you will be deaf for the rest of the day.

The crowds really take the fun out of it. I easily spotted 50 boats that morning and very few dolphins – if any. The rare moments when a dolphin did show, every boat immediately raced over to get closer, so a pretty terrible experience overall.

Fortunately, our "captain" had to fix some motor failure along the way which brought us there late and so we stayed much longer than anyone else.

THAT's – when the dolphins started to appear in large numbers!

They obviously avoided the noisy crowds, but were happy to show with just a few boats around.

So try to arrange a tour a little later than everyone else and you might actually get to see some dolphins....

Diving & Snorkeling

Diving and snorkeling are the biggest activities on the North and East Coast - aside from hiking trips into the mountains. Most accommodations offer diving and snorkeling tours, including trips to remote *Menjangan Island* in the *West Bali National Park*. No need to pre-reserve, you can book when you arrive.

Speaking of accommodations - a beautiful and reasonably priced luxury villa resort with a stunning coast line and an amazing pool is **Puri Bagus Lovina** (PuriBagusLovina.com). A beautiful spot for a few days and a good base to explore the region.

Day Trips

Lovina is a good, central base for a number of wonderful day trips, including:

* Gitgit Waterfall
* Munduk
* Twin Lakes
* Bedugul Lake
* Jatiluwih Rice Terrace
* Cocoa Grounds
* Buddhist Monastery
* Banjar Hot Springs

More on those in the next chapter....

Chapter 8 - Northern Mountains

Gitgit Waterfall - Munduk - Twin Lakes - Bedugul Lake - Jatiluwih Rice Terrace

All five destinations are stunning, relatively uncrowded (except *Gitgit*), and must-sees on your trip around Bali.

The mountain scenery is breath taking offering ever new gorgeous vistas and hiking opportunities.

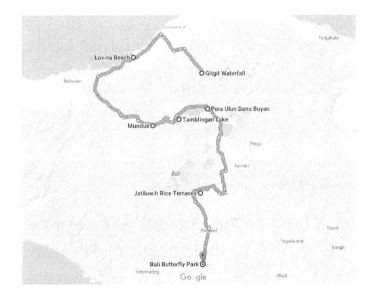

There are two routes to combine all the above sites. You either start with Gitgit or Munduk - and you can also use this route for your return journey back to the South.

Definitely the most stunning of all return options!

Gitgit Waterfall

I saw *Gitgit* on my way to Lovina since it's an easy loop and later took the route via Munduk as part of my return trip back to the South - after visiting the *West Bali National Park*.

Gitgit is the most famous water fall in Bali and can get a little crowded occasionally. It is 300m above sea level and comprised of 3 different falls, all with separate parking lots, but flowing from the same watershed.

Munduk

The drive up to Munduk into the mountains is spectacular! - One of the most beautiful vistas in all of Bali!

If you love mountains, a stay in Munduk should be part of your itinerary.

Munduk is a small village, quite busy, but pleasant, and the scenery is one of a kind. A number of coffee plantations along the way invite to tasting and tours and the region is a hiker's paradise with numerous gorgeous routes and a well regulated tour guide system that lets you choose between in-depth guide or just someone to point the way. There is also a waterfall to enjoy.

If you can, try to book accommodations along the mountain side - a beautiful simple guesthouse with gorgeous mountain views is **Aditya Guesthouse** (SassyZenGirl.com/Aditya-Munduk)

At approx. 800m above sea level, Munduk's climate is cooler and misty. AC won't be as important, and be sure to bring a sweater or jacket for the evenings.

Twin Lakes

As you climb along gorgeous, dizzying serpentines to ever more fantastic views, you eventually arrive at *Twin Lakes*.

Two volcanic lakes - *Buyan* and *Tamblingan* - adjoining each other. Beautiful turquoise waters and mountain scenery - absolutely stunning!

Tamblingan Nature Recreation Park offers some wonderful hiking, canoeing and camping options. You can also hike to the lake from Munduk.

Tamblingan Lake is considered to have healing powers according to local mythical lore and the area is home to several temples. "Tamba" means medicine, and "elingang" spiritual.

Bedugul: Temple Unun Danu at Lake Bratan

Soon after, you reach *Bedugul Lake* with *Unun Danau Bratan Temple,* a famous photo op that you often see on postcards - and... the cover of this book...

Another volcanic lake with the misty tops of *Mount Bratan* making for a gorgeous setting.

The gardens are lovely and you can spend some enjoyable time there without having to rush away from the crowds.

The *Bali Botanical Gardens* offer a pleasant way to spend an afternoon and stroll through beautiful gardens and the nearby wooden hills. *Bali Treetop Adventure Park* (BaliTreeTop.com) invites to zip lining.

Bedugul is "Bali's fruit and vegetable garden" thanks to rich volcanic soil. A particular attraction are strawberries and pick-your-own strawberry farms.

Local produce can also be found on the surrounding markets, with *Pancasari Market* being the nicest less touristy option - locals actually shop there - vs. overpriced tourist trap for day trippers from the South: *Candikuning Market*.

Jatiluwih Rice Terrace

The most stunning vista on this trip for me was *Jatiluwih Rice Terrace*. Absolutely spectacular!

You can take longer hikes through the rice fields. It's a vast area and depending on your fitness (it is quite steep - and rather warm and humid) you can spend several hours just hiking through the most beautiful countryside.

There is a lovely restaurant at the starting point. A beautiful spot to enjoy the view and spend some quiet time.

From there you can either head South via *Magati* = the small country roads and villages - or return to Lovina and continue your journey West.

Bali Butterfly Park

If you continue South from *Jatiluwih*, you will soon pass *Bali Butterfly Park* (BaliButterflyPark.com). Located in the village of *Wanasari*, the park spreads over 3000 square meters.

Bali Butterfly features several enclosed flower garden compounds housing hundreds of butterflies, some of them endangered species.

The park also serves as a research center and conservation site.

Chapter 9 - Lovina Beach to Pemuteran

The road from Lovina to Pemuteran is dotted with a number of lovely spots.

The drive takes about 2 hours, but can easily spread much longer if you include some of the following:

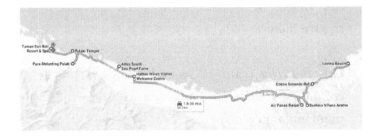

Cocoa Grounds

Located right outside Lovina, *BT Cocoa* (NorthBaliAlliance.com/BT-Cocoa), is the largest cocoa producer in Northern Bali offering a fun stop along the way with some yummy pleasures.

The company actively supports local farmers with training and support to create long term sustainable growth and quality products. A great concept!

Buddhist Monastery: Brahma Vihara.Arama

This Buddhist monastery beautifully set in the mountains provides breathtaking views and serene, peaceful surroundings. It is the biggest Buddhist temple in Bali.

Banjar Hot Springs

Nearby *Banjar Hot Springs* (BanjarHotSpring.co.id) offers a large hot springs pool (38 C, 26% sulfur), a children's pool and Japanese massage showers. Built by Japanese settlers, the springs are surrounded by lush rain forest inviting to leisurely strolls.

You can also get spa services and enjoy some culinary delights.

Overall, touristy, yes, but not too crowded and a nice side stop for a refreshing bath....

Both the monastery and Banjar are not right off the road. You have to drive a little inland, so plan at least 30 min each way for the drive back and forth to the main highway.

Hatten Winery

Vineyards are not necessarily what you would expect in Bali, but yes, they do grow wine here and *Hatten's Winery* (HattenWines.com) is quite famous in the region.

The vineyards are about 15 minutes outside of Pemuteran, and you can go for a free wine tasting which is fun.

Hatten offers a variety of flavors - including some Australian grown grapes - and I quite liked the *Alexandria*.....

The winery also supports the effort of **Ratu Lestari Alami**, (NaturalLightCandlEco.com/Category/Save-The-Bees) an organization that tries to repopulate North Bali with bees. A beautiful, and much needed program - and you can find **more info here.**

Atlas Pearls

The third in the menagerie of interesting and unusual attractions on your way to Pemuteran is **Atlas Pearls** (NorthBaliAlliance.com/Atlas-Pearls-2) an active pearl farm right on the water, famous for their "South Sea Pearl".

You can participate in a free tour with video introduction into pearl farming and exploration of their facilities, and finish the tour in the showroom, featuring beautiful pearl jewelry and perfumes.

A unique feature at *Atlas Pearls* - and one I especially liked - is the fact that all pearl farmers employed by the company are women, very unusual in this otherwise, male dominated industry.

Turtle Hatchery

A wonderful project by *Reef Seen Divers Resort* (ReefSeenBali.com) in Pemuteran to help revive the rapidly declining turtle population in Bali. You can visit the hatchery and also sponsor and release a junior turtle. A beautiful idea, well worth of support and purely non-profit: ReefSeenBali.com/more/Turtles.php

Award Winning Coral Reef Restoration Project

Pemuteran features another eco friendly attraction: a coral reef restoration project that has enjoyed amazing success since 2000 and is run by the *Karang Lestari Foundation*. *Taman Sari Bali Resort* (SassyZenGirl.com/ Taman-Pemuteran) provides easy access, but you don't have to stay there to see the corals.

In 2012, the project was awarded the *Equator Prize* by the *United Nations Development Program (UNDP)* as the world's largest, longest running and most successful coral reef restoration project!

Based on a technique called "Biorock", the project is making use of the fact that low voltage current in seawater causes dissolved minerals to crystallize and form structures similar to limestone where coral larvae can settle and grow.

Biorock technology has been further developed to adapt to coastal environments and the results can easily be observed just a few meters off the coast of Pemuteran.

You can see the corals either snorkeling or diving, and you can also adopt a baby coral and support the project. More info here: BioRockBali.webs.com

Monkey Temple

Pura Pulaki is the main temple for Pemuteran and only 25m away from the ocean. It commemorates the arrival of the Javanese saint Nirartha to Bali in the early 16th century. It is said that when Nirartha entered the forest of Pulaki he was escorted by monkeys. Out of respect for the monkeys he built *Pulaki Temple* and the monkeys became its guardian.

If there is no ceremony (and there often is....) you can climb the stairs all the way up to the main compound and enjoy amazing views of the ocean and surrounding jungle.

Melanting Temple

Located on the slopes of Mount Pulaki, this temple is the most secluded in the region and surrounded by lush rain forest, tropical jungle and several vineyards.

It is a beautiful spot and much less crowded than a lot of other temples.

Hike up Beratan Mountain

A lovely 60 minute hike, especially nice at sunset with wonderful views of the bay and over to the Java volcanoes. At the top, you'll find a small meditation center and a rest area, offering reprieve for body, mind and spirit.

2 nice, simple Guesthouses in Pemuteran are **Pande** (SassyZenGirl.com/Pande-Guesthouse) & **Trijaya** (SassyZenGirl.com/Trijaya-Pemuteran). Both under $20, with AC, ensuite bathroom, breakfast, wifi.

Chapter 10 - West Bali National Park

The scenery and vegetation change rather abruptly once you leave Pemuteran and enter the *West Bali National Park*.

Founded in 1941, *Bali Barat National Park* as it's also called, spreads over 19,000 ha. Vegetation includes monsoon forest, mangroves, rain forest, savanna, sea grass, coral reefs, sandy beaches as well as shallow and deep sea waters.

The Park has over 175 species of plants, 14 of which are endangered like cendan, or sandalwood. The park is also a bird watcher's paradise with 160 different species to enjoy and discover.

Menjangan deer ("Menjangan" = "deer" in Indonesian) - are a frequent and welcome sight and of course, monkeys are never far away....

There are walking paths for hiking and you can also go biking and horse back riding - and kayaking.

The most famous spot in the park is *Menjangan Island* with beautiful coral reefs for snorkeling and diving.

The most wonderful spot to explore the park from is *The Menjangan Resort* which was one of the most beautiful, secluded places I ever visited on my travels -

in particular, the Beach Villas. You can see a scenic video on my travel blog at: SassyZenGirl.com/Menjangan-Luxury-Resort-Bali-National-Park.

A less expensive base for exploring the park is nearby Pemuteran with a wide range of accommodations in all price groups. You can book tours through your place of accommodation.

Overall, tours are more expensive up here than in the South, and there are no taxis though motor scooter rentals are easy and very cheap.

PERMITS & GUIDES

Admission to the park is 200,000 IDR (about $15) and you need to hire an official park guide which costs around 300,000 IDR (about $20).

You can book through your hotel or drive out yourself and arrange for a guide at the following two locations inside the park:

- *Cekik* near Gilimanuk and the Java ferry
- *Labuhan Lalang* where you can also catch the ferry to Menjangan Island

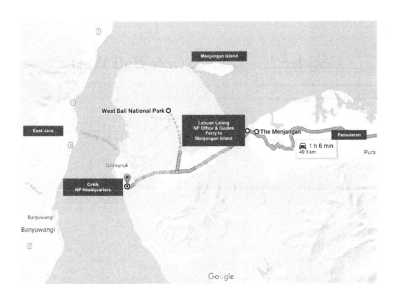

Chapter 11 - East Java & Bali West Coast

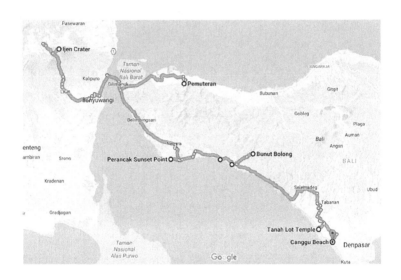

The "Green Crater" in Eastern Java

From Pemuteran you can book a day trip into Java and the volcanoes - a fantastic experience that shows yet another facet of this fascinating region.

Eastern Java lies right across a narrow waterway from the Westernmost coast of Bali, just past the National Park.

The most amazing Indonesian volcano is *Ijen Crater* (2,600m/8,660ft), the "Green Crater", a 1-km-wide turquoise-colored, acid crater lake with an active sulphur mine. Absolutely stunning!

It's easy to access, and the trek is about 3km (half of which are a bit steep at times)

Bali West Coast

Medewi Beach

Driving down the West Coast is not as spectacular as other parts of Bali and the highway can be more crowded (relatively speaking...), but if surfing is your passion, then *Medewi Beach* is a must!

Just like the East and North are famous for diving, the Bali West Coast is a mecca for surfers, the other famous spot being Canggu Beach further in the South.

Medewi has a more laid back vibe, the way Bali used to be before tourism overran the South. Even as a non-surfer it's a nice spot to spend a day or two just to chill and enjoy the ocean. Once again, the beaches are black and better walked with firm shoes due to rocks and sea

urchins - and there are cows along the beach (yes, cows…..).

On the way to *Medewi*, there are several lovely spots that invite for a rest and photo ops:

Purancak Temple & Perancak River Boats

This is a little detour (8km) off the highway and offers beautiful vistas and gorgeous historic boats - traditional *Jukung* and *Sampan* boats. They were brought to Bali by the Bugis seafarers who settled at the end of the 17th century.

Purancak Temple is a nearby site and if you aren't "templed out" yet, another lovely stop.

Rambut Siwi Temple

Closer to *Medewi,* follows this lovely, less-visited temple right by the ocean. One of the largest temples in Bali, *Rambut Siwi* offers some quiet retreat and magnificent ocean views.

Sacred Bunut Bulong Tree

A "tree with a hole" as the literal translation goes. Located inland in *Manggissari* in the Medewi area, this sacred tree has a clove plantation on one side and a gorge with lush green tropical forest on the other. A road leads right through the tree.

Tanah Lot Temple

The ocean temple of *Tanah Lot* was for me - and many others…. - one of the few disappointing sites in Bali. It's overcrowded with traffic jams, a classic tourist trap with hundreds of shops and aggressive hawkers harassing you every step of the way and the temple - once you finally get there - is not that impressive. There are much more beautiful ocean temples along the coast - without the crowds.

Every tour guide will try to sell you on *Tanah Lot* tours, but from what I saw, it was by far the worst experience I ever had in Bali, and I would never recommend it to anyone.

As it is along the Western coastal route, I felt I should include it here - but that's one site you can probably skip....

Canggu Beach

Canggu Beach returns us to the touristy South though not yet as overtly crowded and hedonistic as Seminyak or Kuta.

Canggu used to be a quiet, rural area, covered with rice fields, but in recent years a boom of luxury villa construction has replaced beautiful nature with noisy concrete.

The area is famous for surfing and it is one of the more expensive spots in Bali. For a few days of enjoying beach walks and good food, Canggu can be a fun option, but I found the business a bit of a shock after returning from the quiet North - and that is nothing compared to Kuta, Seminyak and Sanur!

An fantastic spot is **Tugu Hotel** (SassyZenGirl.com/ Tugu-Hotel-Bali-Canggu) right on the beach. Not light on the wallet - but a truly unique experience and frequently listed among the "100 Most Beautiful Hotels in the World". Donna Karan and Kate Moss have stayed here, among other celebrities.

Tugu is family run and was founded by an Indonesian Art Collector as a place to display his extraordinary collection - the largest of Indonesian art in the world!

The hotel is basically an elegant museum featuring some of Indonesia's most precious antiques everywhere on the grounds. Each suite is uniquely decorated, and the hotel offers one of the best Indonesian restaurants in

the country - even the Indonesian President orders from here (well, the Jakarta branch anyway....;-).

While most of the South is covered with overcrowded tourist spots, Jimbaran in the southwest has some lovely quiet areas and beaches - also South Ungasan. A famous site in that area is *Uluwatu Temple* atop breath taking ocean cliffs with a **rambunctious Macaques** colony to enjoy…..

Final Words

There you have it….

A "quick" overview over one of the most beautiful - and varied - islands in the world.

I hope you will have a better sense now what to explore further and how to plan your trip.

Wherever you go (except the crowded tourist South), Bali will be wonderful and enchant you with her lightness of being, her joyfulness and deep stillness. It is a magical place, and I wish you wonderful travels and amazing adventures in this paradise.

Until then….Blissful Travels!

Gundi Gabrielle
SassyZenGirl.com

As a reminder - all resource links, photos & maps can be found here:
SassyZenGirl.com/Bali-Photos

More SassyZenGirl Yummies

COURSES

SassyZenGirl's Blogging Bootcamp
SassyBlogBootcamp.com

FREE Masterclass:
POWER MARKETING BLUERPRINT
DreamClientsOnAutopilot.com

Award Winning
INFLUENCER FAST TRACK
Series

#1 Bestselling
BEGINNER INTERNET MARKETING
Series
"The Sassy Way... when you have NO CLUE!"

#1 *Bestselling*
TRAVEL BOOKS

Score FREE Flights, Rental
Cars & Accommodations.
Dramatically reduce Airfares.
Get paid to Travel & START a
DIGITAL NOMAD BIZ
you can run from anywhere
in the world!

ZEN TRAVELLER
BALI
A QUICK GUIDE

Explore the "real" Bali…
The quiet, magical parts
far away from the
tourist crowds…

About the Author

Gundi Gabrielle, aka *SassyZenGirl*, loves to explain complex matters in an easy to understand, fun way. Her *"The Sassy Way...when you have NO CLUE!!"* series has helped thousands around the world conquer the jungles of internet marketing with humor, simplicity and some sass.

A 11-time #1 Bestselling Author, Entrepreneur and former Carnegie Hall conductor, Gundi employs marketing chops from all walks of life and loves to help her readers achieve their dreams in a practical, fun way. Her students have published multiple #1 Bestsellers outranking the likes of Tim Ferris, John Grisham, Hal Elrod and Liz Gilbert.

When she is not writing books or enjoying a cat on her lap (or both), she is passionate about exploring the world as a Digital Nomad, one awesome adventure at a time.

She has no plans of settling down anytime soon.

Made in the USA
Middletown, DE
29 December 2022

20716647R00066